THEN *&* NOW

# TROY

*To Vic,*
*ENJOY YOUR*
*SECOND CITY*
*♡ D*

*Opposite:* Edwin Emerson contemplates Troy and his future in this self-portrait taken on Mount Ida on April 25, 1862. From his viewpoint, he can see downtown Troy, and to the north Troy University's towers reach for the sky in this photograph taken as part of his involvement with the Amateur Photographic Exchange Club. On May 10, a few weeks after this photograph was taken, he would have seen most of downtown Troy—right up to the university—burned in a disastrous fire that claimed more than 500 buildings.

THEN & NOW

# TROY

## Don Rittner

*To Christopher, Kevin, Jackson, Jason, and Jennifer*

Copyright © 2007 by Don Rittner
ISBN 978-0-7385-5494-5

Library of Congress control number: 2007927918

Published by Arcadia Publishing
Charleston SC, Chicago IL, Portsmouth NH, San Francisco CA

Printed in the United States of America

For all general information contact Arcadia Publishing at:
Telephone 843-853-2070
Fax 843-853-0044
E-mail sales@arcadiapublishing.com
For customer service and orders:
Toll-Free 1-888-313-2665

Visit us on the Internet at www.arcadiapublishing.com

*On the front cover*: These images show Market Square looking north down River Street. The Boardman Building on the right housed the Troy Museum and it was here that *Uncle Tom's Cabin* was first performed in America for over 100 consecutive nights in 1852. The 1880s photograph shows a busy downtown with shoppers, trolleys, and wagons, along with Franklin and Chatham Squares at the end of the street. On the left is the building of the *Troy Observer*, a local newspaper published between 1879 and 1927. This entire section of Troy was leveled during the 1970s. The contemporary image is the identical view, taken in 2007. (Vintage photograph courtesy of the Rensselaer County Historical Society; contemporary photograph courtesy of Don Rittner.)

*On the back cover*: Children are hanging about the "stage" entrance peeking in, in an alley in back of a moving picture theater on First Street. This photograph was taken at 10:30 p.m. The little tot on the right said he was five years old. The image was taken by Lewis Wickes Hine in February 1910. (Courtesy of the Library of Congress, National Child Labor Committee records.)

# CONTENTS

# ACKNOWLEDGMENTS

Books like this one are only possible because certain people had the vision to collect and preserve images of the past. Special thanks go to the following people for the use of photographs for this book: Rich Herrick and the Troy German Hall Association; Chris Hunter, archivist for the Schenectady Museum; Jim Shaughnessy, author of *Delaware & Hudson* and *The Rutland Road*, for great railroad pictures; Tom and Ray Clement from Clements Frame Shop at 201 Broadway in downtown for a number of great early-20th-century photographs available for framing, especially from their Louis Albert Birkmayer Collection (about 1910–1916); the staff at Rensselaer County Historical Society, excellent caretakers of the county's rich history; Marjory Roddy and St. Paul's Episcopal Church; and John E. Swanteck, director, Watervliet Arsenal Museum. I am indebted to my editor, Pam O'Neil, for keeping me on course.

# INTRODUCTION

Troy, once one of the most powerful and wealthiest cities in America, has undergone the proverbial rise and fall of any human endeavor. Situated on the fertile floodplain of the Hudson River, 150 miles north of New York City, Troy had meager beginnings as a series of feudal farms in the 17th century, expanding to a mercantile village after the Revolution, and then exploding as a supercity with the invention of the collar-and-cuff industry and a diversity of iron and steel products that lasted well into the 20th century.

At its peak, the Troy brand was known worldwide on products that ranged from cast-iron stoves, bells, horseshoes, rail, collars, cuffs, shirts, and a host of other useful items. It was the fourth-wealthiest city in America, boasting more Tiffany windows than any other city of its size. It provided major contributions during the Civil War by producing hull plates for the USS *Monitor*. It was the home of American icon Uncle Sam, a real-life Trojan named Sam Wilson who packed meat for the troops during the War of 1812. A city of inventors and go-getters, Troy never lost an opportunity to create and prosper.

All of this changed beginning in the 1950s, as industry and population began to flee southward and westward. After its fall from power, the city entered a period of collective low esteem. It resorted to the demolition of complete neighborhoods and business districts in an attempt to improve the old city and compete with the suburbs and shopping malls that welcomed the fleeing population. Instead of attracting people, however, hundreds of families were forced to move out as their neighborhoods were replaced with bridges that created dead zones and that separated one part of the city from the other. The downtown area was wiped clean. All that remained were the empty shells of Troy's former eminence, and the city spiraled to near bankruptcy in the 1990s.

Troy has begun a renaissance in the current century. An influx of artists, professionals, and others have rediscovered the "Tiffany City," purchased and restored homes, created new businesses, and contributed to the new social and economic climate. The historic city is reemerging, although much work remains to be completed before Troy can be considered fully reborn.

This book can be viewed as a lesson, a wake-up call, a warning against the continued whittling away of the remaining historic fabric of the city. On page after page, fine old neighborhoods and solid buildings that once graced Troy fall to the wrecking ball, often without a plan to replace them with anything permanent. The citizens who inhabited the homes and worked in the businesses disappear, and the city ceases to prosper and evolve.

The old proverb "to the victor go the spoils" was coined by Trojan William L. Marcy, New York's governor in 1833. Perhaps it is time again for Trojans to become victors by preserving and honoring their past. Troy is still a city of historic beauty with many architectural gems, and every effort must be used to preserve them.

Don Rittner
May 2007

CHAPTER

# 1

# CONGRESS STREET
# CORRIDOR

Congress Street was a major east–west thoroughfare before the superhighways were built. This view from atop a building shows Congress Street from Fourth Street to Eighth Street, and College Avenue, running to the top of the hill. In this *c.* 1880 photograph, the "Towers of Troy," built as Troy University, later St. Joseph's Provincial Seminary, can be seen rising from the top of the Eighth Street hill. The Towers of Troy was a major landmark until Rensselaer Polytechnic Institute (RPI) tore it down for a new library in 1976. Eighth Street and College Avenue are seen here being newly populated by homes, while lower Congress is an assortment of retail establishments, hotels, and restaurants.

11

This historic and now-vanished view looks down Congress Street hill (west) just above Eighth Street on the right where the Troy Pie Shop truck is parked. The photograph, taken on September 4, 1926, shows the area in the lower center of the picture that became public housing, known as the Ahern Apartments, for returning war veterans in the early 1950s. The tower of the Second Presbyterian Church on Second Street can be seen in the distance. Ferry Street, also gone, is to the left out of view.

This view looks southeast up a cobblestoned Congress Street hill from short Seventh Avenue on September 4, 1926. This street was lined with Federal- and Greek Revival–era homes until the 1970s, when urban renewal replaced the whole area with grass. Hundreds of families were displaced.

Here is another historic view of Congress Street at the short Seventh Avenue intersection, looking southeast, at a view that no longer exists. The May 24, 1937, photograph was taken when the new General Electric Novalux Luminaries streetlight system was put in place (pole on the right).

A view of the Troy Day Home looking east from Congress Street at Seventh Avenue shows the old Tibbits Mansion that was converted into the day home in 1861. The day home was founded in 1858 and was the oldest day nursery in the United States. Incorporated in 1861, it was the first incorporation in New York State comprised solely of women. The day home provided 100–150 preschool-age children with some basic education, taught handicrafts, and had meals and on-site medical examinations and care. It is now a parking lot for government workers.

Fresh-air buses take kids from the day home to the countryside in 1916. Buses were supplied by the W. H. Lee Moving Company. The building at the top right of the photograph is the Gale Chapel and School built by E. Thompson Gale in honor of his son in 1879. This building was designed by Marcus Cummings, a well-known local architect. The school averaged 100 attendees during the 1880s. Only the retaining wall remains, and the day home and chapel/school is now a parking lot for the building to the left, which is the old Troy High School, later converted to School 5 elementary school, when the high school moved. It is now used as the Rensselaer County government center.

A view looking west down the Congress Street hill shows a very active city in the *c.* 1890 photograph. The Congress Hotel, built in 1848, stands next to the Congress Street train tunnel, which ran under the hill, north and south, to Ferry Street. The First Baptist Church steeple is evident, as are many businesses and homes that once lined the street. Bumstead Chevrolet used the hotel for years, and parts of the old hotel were evident (paneled walls and so on) inside the sales offices. The building is now used for training, but the buildings on the other side of the street have been razed.

The northwest corner of Fifth Avenue and Congress Street has not escaped demolition. The vacant lot used to house the Gross Department Store along with Charlie's Hot Dogs and Myer's newsroom, which were torn down in the 1970s. The old Goldstone store is now the Famous Lunch. In 1932, the Quick Lunch, now Famous Lunch, opened its doors for the first time at 111 Congress Street. On August 28, 1958, a local marine, 20-year-old Cpl. Gordon Gundrum, stationed at the U.S. embassy in Moscow, Russia, had to have his Troy hot dogs. Several dozen dogs were flown to the embassy by KLM Royal Dutch Airlines and were served for lunch that day to Gundrum and the U.S. ambassador at his 54th birthday celebration. The news of "Operation Hot Dogs" made the national and local newspapers, and so the Quick Lunch became world famous. Today Famous Lunch sends hot dogs via FedEx to states throughout the United States and around the world.

Some things have never changed in Troy, such as the inside of the Famous Lunch, seen below in the 1940s. Eating here is like taking a step back in time; the inside has not changed in over 50 years. The hot dogs are still just as good.

Growing up in Troy has memories of almost every corner having a store as represented here by Debboli's Fruit Store on the southeast corner of Congress and Third Streets. These family grocery and fruit stores were all over Troy, but now giant supermarkets have taken over. In these old mom-and-pop stores, customers could "run a tab," that is, get groceries without paying until payday. This building has housed a number of retail businesses.

# CHAPTER 2

# COMMERCIAL
# SQUARES AND
# BUSINESS DISTRICTS

The Market Block was so named because of the public market, built in 1840, at the southwest corner of Fulton and River Streets. (The city provided two other public markets for it citizens.) The second floor contained an entertainment room while the first floor had stalls for meats and vegetables sellers. It was sold in 1879 to William Frear, who had already purchased the American Hotel, now called the Frear House, seen here on the left. Prior to a public market, it was a public ship-construction yard. The market building burned on February 18, 1903, and was replaced by the National State Bank building in 1904. The bank building still stands and has had several uses since.

21

A view of the Market Block south at River Street and the corners of Third and Fulton Streets reveals a very busy downtown. The public market is on the right. The Harmony Hall building on the left was built in 1850 and still survives today, as well as a few of the buildings on the west side of River Street. The Brunswick dairy wagon was making its daily deliveries, as well as other wagon drivers, in the early-1900s photograph.

COMMERCIAL SQUARES AND BUSINESS DISTRICTS

Two teenagers get ready to board the bus at the Boardman Building at the northeast corner of River Street and Fulton Street. The United Cigar Store was an early convenience store, and on Friday and Saturday nights, this corner was packed with teenagers trying to get home before midnight during the 1960s. A parking lot has replaced this busy intersection.

A dramatic view, looking north down River Street from Fulton and Third Streets, highlights the immense change that occurred in the 1960s–1970s urban renewal period. This entire block was demolished. The Boardman Building, on the right in the c. 1910 photograph, was the location where *Uncle Tom's Cabin* was first performed in America in 1852 and ran for more than 100 consecutive nights.

This view of Third Street looking southeast reveals the major changes that have taken place over the years. Earlier buildings were replaced with department stores such as Woolworth's and H. L. Green on this block, only to be demolished in the 1960s for the Uncle Sam Mall project, later called the Uncle Sam Atrium and commonly known as "the glass box." Today the site holds government offices and a few retail establishments.

A view of the northeast corner of Third Street and Broadway shows the Troy Times Building and several retail establishments around 1912. The Troy Times Building was erected in 1871, and the newspaper was a leading local newspaper until the Troy Record purchased it in 1935. It is now part of the site of the Uncle Sam Atrium.

A vibrant and busy downtown Troy in the 1950s is seen here on Third Street between Broadway and Fulton Street looking northwest. The buildings at the end of the street, Peerless and Denby's, were two major department stores along with H. L. Green, Woolworth's, Jupiter's, Kresge's, Grant's, and others. On an average weekend, shoppers had to walk in the streets because there was no room on the crowded sidewalks. Today a person can walk the whole block and never see a soul.

The late-1940s to early-1950s photograph shows Broadway looking east from Third Street up to the RPI approach. The old Quackenbush department store of 1855 on the right was taken over by W. T. Grants, which occupied it during the 1960s. The Broadway corridor was a major retail section of the city at one time.

COMMERCIAL SQUARES AND BUSINESS DISTRICTS

A view looking west up Broadway to Third Street shows one of Troy's many parades in the 1960s. No city loves parades more than Troy, and the city has had one almost every year since the mid-19th century. The building on the right has been replaced as part of the Uncle Sam Atrium.

A busy Christmas scene in downtown Troy, along Third Street from Broadway to Fulton Street, shows many shops offering specials. These were Troy's final days as a busy commercial and retail center as shortly after the c. 1965 photograph was taken, hundreds of buildings were demolished in most parts of the city.

COMMERCIAL SQUARES AND BUSINESS DISTRICTS

The early view of Third Street looking south from Broadway shows the city ready for the Hudson-Fulton celebration of 1908–1909. Buildings were decorated, and thousands turned out for a variety of programs and exhibitions during this time. The block has remained relatively intact and is seeking a revival.

Chatham Square occupied the area between River, Federal, and King Streets and the Rensselaer and Saratoga Railroad bridge (Green Island Bridge). It was a very busy commercial center with the centerpiece being the Manufacturers' National Bank (the building was an early trolley station) that financed the construction of the USS *Monitor* during the Civil War. The Troy–Schenectady railroad, and later trolleys, crossed the bridge and ran down the center of Federal Street and turned to the south (train station) or north (repair yards). The square no longer exists.

COMMERCIAL SQUARES AND BUSINESS DISTRICTS

A look down King Street from Federal Street during the 1913 flood shows a mixed residential-commercial area. King Street entered Columbus Square at the far end of the photograph. A few of the buildings on the right of the photograph still exist.

The view of Chatham Square looking south from the bank building around 1900 is a stark contrast to the present-day photograph, which shows the square and Franklin Square (farther south) completely removed. Hundreds of buildings were demolished here during the 1960s, and even the train tracks (later Troy and Albany Belt Line) are no longer visible. Although the square was removed, nothing has been built in its place.

COMMERCIAL SQUARES AND BUSINESS DISTRICTS

The northeast corner of River and Federal Streets was the location of the Emich and Straub collar and cuff factory and a few retail first-floor businesses such as printing and drugstores in the c. 1909 photograph.

Troy was known as the "Collar City" because it was here that Helen Montague created the first detachable collar in her home in 1827, and Troy became the leading manufacturer of them for over 150 years.

The intersection of Federal and River Streets looking east reveals the Emich and Straaub Collar Company on the left and at the rear of the photograph Grant's Steam Marble Works on Fifth Avenue (then called North Second Street). The hundreds of buildings that were located here all the way east to Eighth Street were demolished in the 1960s.

COMMERCIAL SQUARES AND BUSINESS DISTRICTS

Here can be seen the bridge that literally burned Troy to the ground in 1862. An escaping spark from a locomotive sitting on the Rensselaer and Saratoga Railroad bridge set it ablaze on May 10, 1862. When it was over, 502 buildings in downtown were gone as far east as Eighth Street. Only five lives were lost and the city quickly rebuilt. The bridge that replaced this one collapsed into the river in 1977 with no fatalities and was replaced by the current art deco span.

Franklin Square was the intersection of Fourth, River, and Division Streets (all of Troy's squares were actually rectangles). The view of the square is looking south with River Street on the right and Fourth Street on the left. The photograph was taken shortly before the entire block was razed during the 1960s.

The 1913 view of Franklin Square looks west from Grand Street toward the river. Troy had frequent floods until the state created flood controls in the upper Hudson River later in the 20th century. The quoins (rectangular plates at the corner of a building) of the Manufacturers' National Bank (then Troy City National Bank), seen on the left, represent the only building still standing.

This view looks northwest from Franklin Square toward Chatham Square during one of Troy's many parades, around 1918. Trolleys and wagons are not concerned for the parade participants as they march north down River Street toward Market Square. Burleigh Lithography occupied a building on the left and made aerial panorama (bird's-eye view) drawings of many New York State cities, except Troy.

COMMERCIAL SQUARES AND BUSINESS DISTRICTS

A military parade marches south down Fourth Street at Franklin Square around 1918. The Trojan steam fire engine station is seen on the right along with the Houson Printing Company and Wolf's Hotel.

A close-up of the east side of Fourth Street at Franklin Square shows Curley's Hotel and Restaurant at the corner of Grand Street with the Trojan fire station decked out in banners during a celebration around 1910.

COMMERCIAL SQUARES AND BUSINESS DISTRICTS

Seen here is upper Fourth Street as it enters Franklin Square to the north in 1913. Many of the buildings on the east, right side, of the street still remain today while those on the left were replaced with a parking garage and a hotel.

The east side of Fourth Street from Fulton Street to Franklin Square reveals a busy street with the Troy Automobile Exchange in the middle of the block and the College Inn. The west side of the block was razed, and a parking lot now exists in its place. The alley on the left was known as Museum Place, and it ran behind the Boardman Building, which had a museum in it during the 19th century.

COMMERCIAL SQUARES AND BUSINESS DISTRICTS

A view of Franklin Square at River Street was taken looking north toward the square in 1913. The Manufacturers' National Bank on Chatham Square can be seen in the center of the photograph and a sign for the *Knickerbocker Press*, an Albany newspaper, is on top of a building in the center. An early Wells and Coverly clothes store can be seen on the right. This view no longer exists.

Shown is a busy east side of River Street just south of Franklin Square to Market Square in the mid-1960s shortly before urban renewal demolished these buildings. What is alarming to realize is that these blocks of retail and commercial buildings were in use when the city decided to demolish them with no real plan to replace them with anything better.

The west side of River Street between Franklin Square and Market Square during a parade around 1915 reveals the many commercial buildings that lined the street and that were removed during urban renewal. The area is now a little-used park.

Washington Square is located between Broadway and River and Second Streets and was renamed Monument Square after the Soldiers and Sailors Monument was built in 1891 to commemorate the Civil War. The monument is 93 feet tall and the *Call to Arms* statute is 13 feet tall. Built in 1828, the Mansion House (a hotel) in the background was replaced by the Hendrick Hudson Hotel in 1925 and now serves as government offices.

COMMERCIAL SQUARES AND BUSINESS DISTRICTS

# RAILROAD DAYS

The block around Union Street, Broadway, Fulton Street, and Sixth Avenue was Troy's railroad hub centered in the Troy Union Station that was built in 1854. It burned in the great fire of 1862, was rebuilt, and was then torn down in 1903 for a Beaux-Arts-style station that lasted until 1958. Troy was the center for the Rensselaer and Saratoga (1835), Troy and Schenectady (1842), Troy and Greenbush (1845), and Troy and Boston (1852) Railroads. Later these were consolidated into the New York Central and Boston and Maine Railroads. Trojans loved their trains, and they operated throughout the city as revealed in the next set of photographs. Here the *Chippewa* is ready to depart south, crossing Broadway. RPI is at the top in this *c.* 1890 photograph.

On May 10, 1862, fire swept throughout downtown Troy and destroyed over 500 buildings, including the train station that had been built only eight years before. The view of the ruined station and city was taken from Eighth Street, looking west with Seventh Avenue and burned-out buildings seen below it.

The new Troy Union Station was built in 1903 and is the station most living Trojans remember. Hotels, restaurants, and shops surrounded the station, as did collar and cuff and engineering companies. A classical-design subway went under the station and the many tracks so riders could enter the trains going north or south on the east side of Sixth Avenue and the tracks.

The Congress-Ferry Street train tunnel began here at State Street and went under Congress Street and Ferry Street exiting on the south side of Ferry Street. Sixth Avenue occupied both sides of the tracks with cars going south on the right side of the photograph and cars moving north down the left side of the 1913 photograph. The tunnel still exists, but the entrances have been filled in, and there is rumor that there may be rolling stock in the abandoned tunnel.

Here is an image that can never be seen again, an Albany train exiting the Congress-Ferry Street tunnel and heading south in August 1957. The Ahern Apartments, now razed, were built for the returning Korean War veterans and later served to house the economically disadvantaged until they were razed a few years ago.

RAILROAD DAYS

Ready to travel are cars full of iron ore (magnetite) from the Republic Steel mine at Lyon Mountain as they pass beneath tower No. 2 of the Troy Union Railroad on March 12, 1955, and on their way through the Troy station to the Republic Steel blast furnace in South Troy in a Delaware and Hudson Railroad (D&H) transfer move.

A view of Troy Union Station from tower No. 1 looking north shows seven pairs of tracks and people ready to board. Every 20 minutes the Capital District's Belt Line trains would stop here and take anyone to Albany and back. The view taken at 6:30 a.m. on March, 12, 1955, is showing a New York Central locomotive on track No. 3 waiting for the arrival of the D&H southbound *Montreal Ltd.* to be forwarded to New York.

This view is of a train, engine No. 422, coming into Troy Union Station under tower No. 1, from the south and through the Congress-Ferry Street tunnel, which can be seen in the background. A truck is crossing the tracks at State Street near the police station.

Pictured is a view of a New York Central train, NYC E-8 No. 4059, heading south to New York City pulling the Laurentian train No. 144 from Montreal via the D&H to Troy under tower No. 1 in June 1950.

A New York Central train, No. 8343, is plowing through snow heading south just north of Grand Street on February 18, 1958. Snow does not seem to slow this one up.

*Green Mountain Flyer* of the Rutland Railroad is arriving, from Montreal via a western Vermont route, in Troy and coming down Sixth Avenue near Grand Street.

A northbound
D&H Laurentian
No. 35 leaves Troy
and is passing tower
No. 3 on Fifth
Avenue as it heads
for the Hudson
River bridge, Green
Island, and north to
Montreal, behind
elephant-eared
4-6-2 No. 608 in
June 1949.

This view shows a Boston and Maine passenger engine on the turntable on May 22, 1957, at the Boston and Maine yards at Middleburg Street and Sixth Avenue. All that remains today is the roundhouse. Mount Olympus is seen in the background.

Troy's railroad era ended with the tearing down of the Troy Union Station on November 20, 1958. The site was used as a parking lot until a new building was erected to house the county welfare offices.

# CHAPTER 4

# NEIGHBORHOODS, VIEWS, AND STREETSCAPES

Shown is Troy's riverside from the Green Island Bridge to the Congress Street bridge (farther south) in April 1948. Barges line the shore waiting for the canal to open. Troy's streetscapes and neighborhoods have been drastically altered in many parts of the city. None of the buildings pictured survived the wrecking ball, and parts of the riverfront have been turned into a park.

A contrasting view from the Green Island Bridge looking north along the riverfront reveals an altered riverfront. This was part of the center of the collar-and-cuff industry with Cluett, Peabody and Company in the center of the photograph. Various proposals have been made in recent years to redevelop the riverfront.

Looking north, River Street, from State Street to Congress Street, contained some of Troy's oldest buildings. The city had its beginnings not far from here at Ferry and River Streets. The building at the corner belonged to one of the local steamship companies, and behind it at the steamboat landing, passengers could take a steamboat to New York City. During the urban removal period of the 1960s and 1970s, the city decided to replace these historic buildings with a parking garage.

Looking east at the corner of State and Fourth Streets one can see the "Towers of Troy," the former St. Joseph's Provincial Seminary. Originally built as Troy University, it was sold to Catholic priest Rev. Peter Havermans in 1864, and it opened in 1864 with 60 students. In 1908, the Sisters of St. Joseph purchased it as a provincial house and novitiate, and RPI purchased it later and tore it down for a library. The Methodist church can be seen on the corner of State Street and Fifth Avenue.

NEIGHBORHOODS, VIEWS, AND STREETSCAPES

The Fifth Avenue Hotel at the corner of Fifth Avenue and Fulton Street was a landmark for many years until it burned. The building in the middle is the Wheeler and Wilson Manufacturing Company that made some of America's first sewing machines and became the standard for the collar, cuff, and shirt makers in Troy. The Costa family, who purchased the building in the early 1970s, found hundreds of steel sewing needles in the floorboards, and one of the sewing machines was donated to the Smithsonian Institution. The building to the left made stove patterns for the many cast-iron stove makers in Troy.

A view of Fourth Street shows the northeast corner. During the 19th century, it was a residential block. In the early 1900s, it was converted for commercial purposes. Proctor's Theater, which opened in 1914 as a vaudeville house, and the New York Telephone Company building can be seen in the contemporary image. Both of these structures replaced several mansions.

NEIGHBORHOODS, VIEWS, AND STREETSCAPES

Shown in the early view, looking west, is a section of Federal Street and Sixth Avenue that no longer exists. The large building on the right is Wagar's Ice Cream factory, originally built as a factory for collars and cuffs housing the C. H. McClellan Company and Joseph Bowman and Sons collar factory in 1903.

The early photograph features a lovely streetscape that has been lost. Looking south from Federal Street, it shows Fifth Avenue, which was known as the Tiffany of streets. The beautiful brownstone mansions stood until the 1960s, when many of them were torn down. The Fifth Avenue Presbyterian Church can be seen in the background, and the intersection of Grand Street is two buildings up from the church.

NEIGHBORHOODS, VIEWS, AND STREETSCAPES

A complete neighborhood on Grand Street east from Sixth Avenue to Eighth Street was razed and later replaced with senior citizen apartment buildings featuring a lot of green space. Some urban designers believe that a city should keep its green space confined to public parks, which can be accessed by the entire population.

One of Troy's premier collar-and-cuff companies was the Earl and Wilson Collar and Cuff factory on the southwest corner of Seventh Avenue and Broadway. Residential homes lined the east side of Seventh Avenue as seen in the *c.* 1903 photograph. The historic Seventh Avenue area from Ferry Street to Hoosick Street no longer exists.

NEIGHBORHOODS, VIEWS, AND STREETSCAPES

This is the opposite side of the street (northwest) from the collar company and reveals a street lined with many homes. Note the domed structure of the railroad station and a railroad car down Broadway in the c. 1899 photograph.

A view down Broadway from the RPI approach shows the link between the city and engineering school. This is the site of an earlier building of the RPI engineering college, the earliest engineering school in the country founded in 1824. The building burned in 1904, and the city erected the RPI approach in 1924 to connect the city to the college (the mayor was a graduate). The RPI gymnasium is on the left, and the Protestant Episcopal Church Home is on the right. The approach was restored by RPI recently; it is, however, no longer a direct walk down to Troy.

Another neighborhood that was leveled is the section of Fulton Street from Eighth Street to Sixth Avenue, looking west. In the c. 1900 photograph, the domed structure on the left is the railroad station, and the Christian church is just before it on the corner of Seventh Avenue. The Tremont House is on the west side of the tracks to the right, and the public market is at the end of Fulton Street.

No other streetscape has gained as much attention in recent years as the Hoosick Street corridor. Once a two-lane residential street, it now has an off-ramp from a bridge and several highway lanes. Blocks of buildings were demolished for the new route, which separates one part of the city from the other.

NEIGHBORHOODS, VIEWS, AND STREETSCAPES

The area around Grand and Federal Streets once was the home of thousands of Trojans. After the wrecking ball came in, two remnants were left, as seen in the photograph taken on April 29, 1970. Only one or two buildings have replaced what was once a thriving neighborhood. John F. Kennedy Towers (two planned but only one built) was built in 1967.

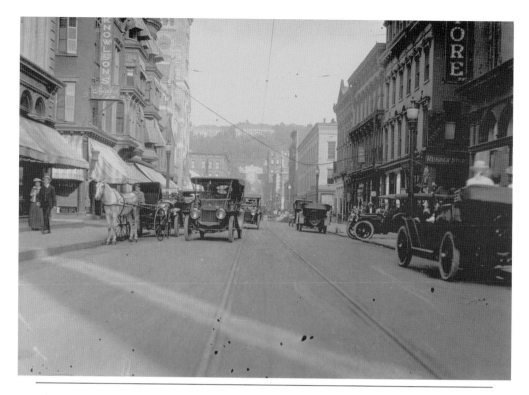

The 1913 view of Broadway from the middle of the block just past Third Street looking east to the RPI approach shows a lively commercial part of downtown. The streetscape has been changed considerably with the addition of a newer post office building and the razing of the buildings to the left for the Uncle Sam Atrium.

NEIGHBORHOODS, VIEWS, AND STREETSCAPES

The 1910–1913 view of the intersection of Fourth Street and Broadway looking west shows a fire truck being drawn past the government building (post office) on a cobblestone street. The old post office was built in 1894 and was replaced with the present one in 1936 as a Works Progress Administration project.

A 1910–1913 view of Broadway, looking east, shows the Sanford and Robinson's Collar Company just before the train station. The little luncheonette on the northwest corner of Fifth Avenue still serves food today.

NEIGHBORHOODS, VIEWS, AND STREETSCAPES

# LANDMARKS

Here is a rare view of the city's first cemetery at the northeast section of State and Third Streets. Gravestones are visible in the photograph from around the 1870s. This land was deeded to the Village of Troy on May 10, 1796, by Jacob D. Vanderheyden "to be used for a public burial ground." More than 200 bodies were taken to Oakwood Cemetery when the land was taken for Troy's city hall in 1875. There are still more graves between the city hall parcel and the Baptist church.

The village burial ground was replaced with Troy's city hall, shown here at the southeast corner of State and Third Streets around 1890. The building was designed by Marcus Cummings, a local architect, and was occupied in 1876 but burned on October 28, 1938. It was converted to Barker Park, and in 1964, the east half of the park was given to St. Anthony's Church, which still occupies the site.

Germania Hall at 134 River Street served the German community until it burned in January 1948, but it was rebuilt as seen here into a three-story building, instead of four, and reopened in September of that year. However, only four years later, on Sunday, March 30, 1952, a ceremony commemorating the hall's closing was held. The city decided that it would build a government-subsidized, low-income housing project, the Taylor Apartments, on the site, and Germania Hall, Lew's Bakery and Deli, and others would be demolished. The Germania hall is now in the Lansingburgh section of the city. Lew's Bakery and Deli moved up one block north of Congress Street and was popular into the 1960s.

Yes, Virginia, there really was an Uncle Sam, and he lived in Troy. Sam Wilson lived in the house on the left at the corner of short Seventh Avenue and Ferry Street. A meat packer by trade with his brother, Wilson became known as American icon Uncle Sam during the War of 1812, serving meat to the soldiers. His house was standing until the city and the State of New York tore it down in 1976 while the country was celebrating its bicentennial.

The oldest civil engineering school in the country's history, RPI was founded in 1824 by Amos Eaton and Stephen Van Rensselaer in the former Farmer's Bank building at the northwest corner of Middleburg and River Streets. Its sprawling campus at the top of the hill on Eighth Street produces some of the nation's most brilliant people and has undergone a great deal of expansion in the early 21st century.

Troy's genesis started here at the corner of Ferry and River Streets. It was here that Dirck Vanderheyden settled and where his three great-grandsons, Jacob I., Jacob J., and Matthias, divided their farms into building lots. The rest is history. The International Hotel, seen here, is said to have been the original Dirck Vanderheyden building with additions. The site is no longer accessible on foot as an on-ramp and a tunnel entrance from a bridge have been constructed here.

Troy High School, on the west side of Fifth Avenue, was built in 1898 and occupied in 1901. Later it became the Central Grammar School in 1917 and School 5 after that. It was torn down in 1963 and replaced by a parking lot. Today the site is occupied by a parking garage.

Chuckrow's at 93 River Street was the source for fresh chicken. When the Taylor Apartments were built in 1952, it moved a block south and in recent times moved to Latham. It was not an unusual sight to see truckloads of clucking chickens on their way to their fate during the 1960s.

POULTRY · BUTTER · EGGS          JOS. CHUCKROW'S SONS          JOS. CHUCKROW'S S

Another streetscape altered is seen here at Division Street looking west from First Street to the river. On the right is the Congregation Sharah Tephilah Synagogue, and the tall building on the left is the Knowlson and Kelly Machine Shop on the former Matthias Vanderheyden property. Russell Sage College owns most of this area at the present time.

The Warren Hardware store, on the right, had a complete cast-iron facade. This building and the two to the left and the telegraph building to the right were replaced by city hall and its parking lots. Silas Watson Ford worked at the telegraph office and was an amateur paleontologist. At 23, Ford was a leading authority on Cambrian fauna east of the Hudson River. He even had one of his fossils named after him by a leading paleontologist, in 1881. *Fordilla troyensis* is one of the oldest-known bivalves in the world.

Here a 2,000-pound bell is being cast at the Meneely Bell Company on River Street in 1915 for the suffragette movement. Troy was a leading bell maker, and Meneely bells are still heard around the world even though the company has been gone for years. The bell was used in the campaign for women's suffrage and was known as the Justice Bell from the fact that the suffrage movement looked upon a woman's right to vote as a matter of justice. The bell was the brainchild and gift of Katharine Wentworth Ruschenberger of Strafford, Chester County, Pennsylvania, and it was her plan to call attention to the battle for women's suffrage. It duplicated the Liberty Bell, except this one has "establish justice" in the inscription. Meneely also made the duplicate of the original Liberty Bell that hangs in Philadelphia.

Mount Olympus along with Mount Ida were named when the village of Vanderheyden became Troy. The *c.* 1860 photograph shows the railroad bridge, on the right, that burned down Troy's center in 1862. Fifth Avenue was carved through Mount Ida during the later part of the 20th century but still commands a good view of the city from the top.

The marketplace, around 1915, was located at Liberty Square near Fifth Avenue and Hill Street. One of the first public markets was erected here in the early 19th century, and later the Troy Gas Company erected its gasometers and sheds here to supply the city with gas. Located in the city's Little Italy neighborhood, there is a move to make the market area come alive again with active recreation and programs.

Robinson, Church and Company, a wholesale druggist at 201 River Street, was typical of the many types of retail and commercial establishments that made Troy an important city in the 19th century. Now converted to apartments, it exists alongside other notable 19th-century buildings in Troy's Antique District.

Cluett, Peabody and Company was the last shirt company to leave Troy, going to Georgia after being in Troy since 1851. During the 1980s, shoppers could stop in the clearance section and buy Arrow shirts at a bargain. Troy was the birthplace of the collar-and-cuff industry, and Cluett, Peabody and Company was the Tiffany of the industry. *Helen of Troy, N.Y.*, a 1923 Broadway play by George Kaufman and Marc Connelly, was a spoof of the company. It was a big hit and starred Helen Ford, who was born in Troy. The buildings to the right belonged to Fitzgerald Brewery Company, a hometown brew under the Fitz label. The brewery burned on November 1, 1964.

# ACROSS AMERICA, PEOPLE ARE DISCOVERING SOMETHING WONDERFUL. *THEIR HERITAGE.*

Arcadia Publishing is the leading local history publisher in the United States. With more than 3,000 titles in print and hundreds of new titles released every year, Arcadia has extensive specialized experience chronicling the history of communities and celebrating America's hidden stories, bringing to life the people, places, and events from the past. To discover the history of other communities across the nation, please visit:

## www.arcadiapublishing.com

Customized search tools allow you to find regional history books about the town where you grew up, the cities where your friends and family live, the town where your parents met, or even that retirement spot you've been dreaming about.

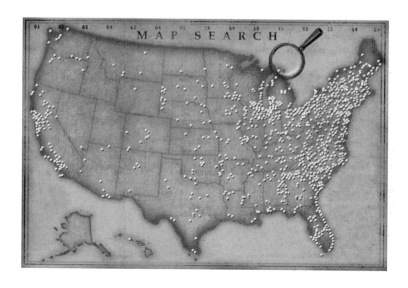